This book is for those who want to live their dream lives, those who can picture it in their minds, make plans to start the journey, but then fail to take any action. Those who are tired of the excuses they've made to put it off until another day.

*Ready, Set, Stop Putting off your dream life* is a compilation of the things I've learned that can help you start taking those steps toward your dream life today. This book will give you the encouragement you need and advice to help you start the journey to your dream life. It's written in layman's terms, not with textbook terminology you don't understand. If you re-read it, it's because you want to, not because you couldn't understand it.

Each chapter has a story, some with humor and some that will make you think. I've found that the best way to understand something is to look around you. If you have questions, all you have to do is look closely at your own circumstances. Lessons are all around us. The answers are there.

After reading this book, I encourage you to start taking a closer look at your own life, at the circumstances surrounding you that are trying to give you the answers you seek. Use them to understand why you think the way you do, and why those thoughts are holding you back. It's time to get ready, set, and stop putting off the life you've been dreaming of.

# ASPIRATION

The definition of "aspiration" in Webster's New World Dictionary is "a strong desire or ambition".

I was reading an article in a magazine recently and one sentence jumped off the page at me. "She would live her life in quiet aspiration." I thought of how sad it was that this woman would "settle" and not pursue her dreams, to live her life wishing she had done the one thing she most wanted to, but never took a step toward it.

I vowed to myself that I wouldn't make that same mistake. I got to thinking about it and a memory from my childhood surfaced. As a child I would watch my mother draw. She drew pictures of women in beautiful dresses while I scribbled in my coloring books. As I got older, the coloring books were replaced with schoolbooks and together we would sit at the table, me with my lessons and her with her dreams. She told me that she used to dream of being a clothes designer and I asked her why she didn't become one. She just smiled and said, "Today, I am". It didn't seem like much of an answer to me at the time and nothing else was ever said about it. She has lived her life happily as a homemaker. When I read this article though, I couldn't help but wonder if she too hadn't lived "a life of quiet aspiration". It took me a few more months and a little help from a fireman to finally understand the answer she gave all those years ago.

One day my eight-year-old grandson came for a visit. On this particular day he walked in and announced, "I'm a fireman!" He didn't say, "When I grow up I want to be a fireman", he said: "I'm a fireman." Suddenly I realized what my mother meant so many years ago when I asked her about becoming a designer. I can still see the smile on her face when she said, "Today, I am", her pencil poised over the page.

I gathered my "fireman" in a warm hug and told him Grandpa and I had some work to do outside and could he watch for fires while we were out there. That idea sounded great, so he grabbed his fireman's hat and his pirate's sword (just in case we came across some pirates) and off we went. He jumped into the red cart (aka fire truck) that I pull behind my riding mower and we headed off into the trees to pick up sticks. Every stop we made he jumped out and fought fires and a few errant pirates. "This is great work, MawMaw!" he told me, smiling from ear to ear. At the end of the day, as I tucked him into bed, he said, "This was the best day ever!" I had to agree with him. Any day you live your dream is the best day ever.

\*\*\*

I've heard so many people say, "I always wanted to learn to play the piano" or "I wish I had gone to college and gotten a degree" or "I always dreamed of being a dancer" or "I always wanted a garden" or "I wish I could paint". There are as many dreams as there are people, diverse and wonderful dreams, and yet so many of us "live our lives in quiet aspiration". Why don't we just jump up and take a chance, one small step toward fulfilling that dream? There are as many excuses as there are dreams. "I don't have the time" or "I'm too old" or "I'm not smart enough" or "My family/friends say it's a waste of time".

Let me tell you something, if it brings you pleasure and fulfillment and gives you a sense of purpose and doesn't harm anyone else, it's not a waste of time. Each small step you take toward your dream enriches you and the world around you.

You're not too old or too stupid, and if you want it bad enough, you'll find the time. You don't have to be the best dancer the world has ever seen or be a rival to Picasso. It's okay to miss a step or hit a wrong note once in a while. It's okay if there are a few weeds in that garden. Just remember that when the music is playing and you're twirling around in the kitchen, you are a dancer. When your fingers move across the keys, you are a pianist. When you get on your knees and dig in the dirt, you are a gardener. When you put the pencil to the page, you are a designer. If you say that no one understands your dream or encourages you, it's okay. They don't have to. It's your dream, not theirs.

Don't spend another day "living a life of quiet aspiration". Take one small step toward your dream and feel your spirit soar. Something happens when you start doing what you were born to do. You know it because you can feel the excitement well up inside

5

you. It spurs you to take the next step, and the next, even when you're scared to. Happiness becomes your normal state. And in the mornings when you wake up, you remember your dream because you've embraced it and you say, "Today, I am." And you take that dream as far as you want it to go. The only one that can stop you – is you. Get up, get busy and live your dream.

*It's only when you wake up that your dream comes to life.*

# CHANGE

I am a "changer". I change things. I change the sheets on the bed, I change lanes when driving on the highway, I make change at work when a customer comes in, I've changed my share of diapers, and, being a woman, I am always free to change my mind. I never really thought much about these changes, they're just a part of life – until one evening when I went to a local fast food restaurant for a quick bite to eat.

After ordering my Number One combo with cheese, I stepped into the lady's room to "freshen up" when I discovered yet another toilet paper dispenser empty. Sitting on top (carefully balanced) was a spare roll of toilet paper. Now with all the "new and improved" items on the market today, the toilet paper industry didn't want to be left behind, so they invented the "mega-roll". I'm sorry, but this thing was bigger than my purse! Well, being the "changer" that I am, I attempted to put the new mega-roll into the mega-roll holder. Try as I might, I could not decipher the secret code needed to open the holder. Maybe it takes a "mega-key" to open. Maybe the employees have to go to a special mega-school to learn how to change them.

While contemplating the options, my mega-roll lost its balance, fell, and proceeded to roll across the floor. I feared it might roll into the view of another customer and disclose my feeble attempts as a changer. After all, I've always prided myself on my ability to change things and this was really shaking my confidence. I grabbed the roll (with both hands) and carefully placed it back on top of the mega-holder, holding my breath as I backed away. Well, being the magnificent changer that I am, I changed stalls. My changer's ego was bruised, but still intact.

As I ate my Number One combo with cheese, I contemplated the possibilities of improving the mega-holder so that the average "changer" could maintain a little dignity and self-confidence. Why don't they invent a toilet paper holder that is built into the wall and when the mega-holder is empty, another roll just falls into place? It would save on storage space since the rolls would be kept in the wall. No mega-keys, no mega-schools, just happy "changers" that can spend their time trying to get the automatic "no-touch" faucets to work. I wonder if there's a class for that too.

*** 

This lighthearted tale, when examined, shows that change is an everyday part of life. By taking a moment to expand on this, I realized that it's not just "life" or "others" that cause changes in our lives.

We have the power to change things ourselves, and we do it every day whether we realize it or not. While replacing a roll of toilet paper is not a life changing event, being aware of the fact that by changing our attitudes or the way we perceive things, we create the world we live in. And we can change it at any time.

But just like changing the "mega-roll", sometimes things don't always work out the way we want them to. We have to back away and take another look. We can approach the change from a different angle, we can tweak it and refine it and try again. Or sometimes, we decide the change isn't what we want after all and we can just let it go.

When it comes to pursuing our dreams and our dream life, change is our constant companion. We have to change our habits. We have to cut out some tv time and practice our craft. We have to sometimes stay up late and get up early. We have to juggle several things at once and learn to manage our time better. It's hard. I know. I do it every day. Changing our habits takes us out of our comfort zones. We have to change the things we do. But instead of feeling like a sacrifice (because I *do* like tv and sleep), it feels more like I'm finally in control of my life. It feels like I'm "doing what matters". I feel confident and happy. And instead of beating myself up for watching that rerun, I respect myself more for having the self-discipline to lay down the remote control, get up, and take another step toward my dream life (even when I'd rather not).

Sometimes it's harder than others to accept all the changes we face in life. But when we choose to embrace change instead of fight it, when we look for the opportunities change can offer us, we can build a better life for ourselves and our loved ones.

Whenever you feel tired of the way things are, if you berate yourself for not having the willpower to do something about the state of your unhappiness, just remember this: *Nothing changes if nothing changes.*

When we decide to take action and follow our dreams, to build the kind of life we've always wanted, *we have to make those changes.* And that changes us. And that's a good thing.

# CHICK FLICK

My daughter and I both had a day off work, so we decided to have a "girl's day out" together; a little shopping, a nice lunch and an afternoon movie. It was a perfect day, one of those that you say "We should do this more often!" when we drag all the bags into the house, complimenting each other on our excellent bargain-finding skills.

When we got to the theater, we chose a chick-flick "No Reservations". Just before the movie started, a young mother climbed up the aisle with her two small children, taking a seat a row or two behind us. The lights went down and we settled in, happily munching our popcorn and slurping our sodas. As the story unfolds, Catherine Zeta-Jones' sister is killed in a car accident and she takes on the responsibility of raising her niece. There's a scene where she finds the little girl asleep on the bed with an open photo album lying beside her. Behind the yellowing plastic sheets of the album are pictures of the little girl and her mother. Catherine Zeta-Jones picks up the album, looks at it a moment, then slowly closes it. It was a moving moment in the story, and the audience could feel the pain they shared. As a mother, I felt my throat constricting and my eyes tearing up.

Silence filled the room with the exception of a sniffle or two. Then I heard the voice of a young child in the audience say "Mommy, I love you." It was one of the children the mother had brought in with her, sitting just a row or two behind us. Undoubtedly, the mother felt that pain along with the rest of us and the child had immediately picked up on it. When the mother didn't respond, the child repeated, a little louder this time: "Mommy – I love you." I heard a whisper from the mother; "I love you, too." At that moment a tear slid down my face and I gave thanks for being a mother. For having the opportunity to know that special kind of love between a mother and her child. For reminding me what life is *really* all about. It was a movie – and a moment – I won't soon forget.

***

We have no reservations about our children. When they're born, something inside us opens up and a new kind of love is born. A selfless love. When we look into their faces, we wonder how we could even profess to knowing love before. Counting their fingers and toes, we're amazed that this little person is even here. "Look how tiny they are" we say when holding their little hand in ours. Feeling the softness of their skin. Holding them in our arms and watching them sleep.

Trying to find the words to describe these feelings is useless. We've experienced no greater joy and received no greater gift in life than a child; and in that moment we are changed forever.

We can apply a "no reservations" rule to other things in our lives as well. Do you have a passion that you've not given birth to yet? A dream for a better life? Is it buried deep inside you waiting to be born? What are you waiting for?

Just as our children learn to crawl before walking, you can "take your first steps" toward living your dream life now. Not sure how? Just stand up, make a decision. Get off the fence and stop using excuses to free you from the chains you've wrapped around yourself. Every link you add trying to justify why you don't take action only serves to make you more miserable and buries it even deeper. Decide you don't want to live like this anymore. *That's* your "first step".

Your next step is to make a "no reservations" promise to yourself that you will work toward that goal determinedly. Even though you may stumble and fall along the way, just like a toddler learning to walk, you will get up and try again. And again. And again.

The next step then is to take action. Start really small. Work yourself up to larger and larger steps. Learn to walk before you run. Think of the simplest thing you can. If a child wants to draw, you give them a box of crayons. If they want to write, you give them a pen. If they want to paint, a paintbrush. Dance? A light to shine on them while they perform. You get the idea.

It's that easy. If you want to be an artist, go buy yourself a box of crayons or a pencil. That's all for one day. Set it where you'll see it often so that when you walk by, you remember that you've taken a step toward your better, more fulfilling life.

That was easy. How many times did you walk by that box of crayons or your new pencil and smile? You took a step and didn't fall. You might have "stumbled" while you were waiting in line to pay for your crayons or pencil, thinking "This is silly", but you hung in there and did it. Good for you.

Using the artist as an example, let's go to the next step. After you bought, say, your pencil, and spent the day enjoying the fact that you finally acted upon your desire for a better life, pick it up and draw something. Make a stick horse, or try drawing a magnificent stallion. Or both. If you go for the stallion and it's not what you hoped it would be you probably felt disappointed and sad that you couldn't draw it better. Somehow, the neck just wasn't right, or the ears were too pointy. You "fell down". So what? Get up and try again. Now is the time that you have to remember your "no reservations" promise.

You didn't tell yourself that you would take action only as long as you could do everything perfectly. You said you had no reservations that you wanted to be an artist and that you would have no reservations about becoming one. You had no reservations about what it would take to get there, that nothing would stop you.

You're going to have setbacks. No one expects a child to just stand up one day and start running around the house. No one expects you to be a masterful artist without practice, persistence and patience. Why would you expect that of yourself?

When a child is learning to walk, they fall. And sometimes they'll lie on the floor crying. You know it's not because they're hurt, it's because they are frustrated and discouraged. You instinctively pick them up and hug them, telling them it's okay and encourage them to try again. That's the same thing you have to learn to do with yourself.

So what if your magnificent stallion looks more like a pointy-eared, skinny-necked stick horse? Try again. And again. And again. Keep moving forward. If you keep trying and you still have that pointy-eared, skinny-necked stick horse, maybe you could draw an owl or a giraffe. Or who knows, there may be someone in this vast world of ours that is searching desperately for a picture of a pointy-eared, skinny-necked stick horse – just like the one you drew.

The point is to not give up. This is when you're going to hear those voices in your head telling you that "You'll never be an artist. That you suck at drawing. That you're just kidding yourself about becoming an artist. Go watch that re-run on tv and forget about it."

But the truth is, you *won't* forget about it. That voice will keep reminding you. "Remember when you tried to draw that magnificent stallion and couldn't? What a loser! Why on earth did you think you could draw? You should have saved the dollar you spent on that pencil and bought an ice cream with it."

You're going to hear those voices now and then. Everyone does. But those who persist in their efforts learn to block those voices out. They become just whispers in the wind as you learn to focus you're thoughts on the relevant things that bring you closer to the kind of life you want to live.

Every one of us is born with a gift. When you nurture it and give it life, you awaken each morning with purpose and determination. And even though you have a long list of things to do, it's okay, because you know that before the day is through, you will create.

I say this with no reservations: You will not only enrich your own life when you give birth to your dreams, but also the lives of others. It all starts with one step. Adopt the mantra: "Every day, one step, then another". Take that first step today. Get off the fence and break those chains. The world is waiting.

# CONTAGION

What is the most contagious thing on the planet? It's not a cold; I *knew* that would be your first answer! It's not the flu virus either, although we really want to avoid catching either one of those. I've been conducting a study (purely non-scientific or medically based), and I've come up with the single most contagious thing on the planet. I actually caught one myself not too long ago from a little girl about three years old. It was a brief contact we made, but just enough for me to catch this contagion. (Everyone knows children carry all sorts of things!) Well, let me just tell you what happened.

I was leaving a local restaurant one evening and as I was walking to the door, a woman was coming in. I waited for her to enter the building and suddenly this little girl walked in. It was a warm day and she had on a little sundress, her round little belly pooched out in front of her. She wore little pink flip-flops with big green flowers pasted on top, and if you looked closely you could see her little toes peeking out from underneath them. She walked into the restaurant, not a care in the world. As a matter of fact, I believe she thought the world was hers that day. She looked up at me, blonde curls and all, and that's when it happened. She smiled.

I caught that smile in the blink of her sparkling blue eyes. Before a thought could cross my mind I was smiling back. She had infected me all right. I didn't stand a chance against her and I just reconciled myself to the fact that I'd have this smile plastered on my face for the rest of the day. I even contemplated the idea of trying to find a pair of pink flip-flops with big green flowers on them for myself.

Even today, when I think about that little girl, that smile comes right back, and if I'm lucky, I'll pass it on to someone else, some poor unsuspecting soul in need of a lift. The great thing about catching a smile is that it makes you feel good, and if you can pass it on to someone else, it makes them feel good too; and it makes you feel even better!

You don't need to call the doctor if you catch a smile, but if for some reason you're just not able to, if you're totally immune to this contagion, you better make yourself an appointment as soon as possible.

***

Let's face it, some days you just don't feel like smiling. You wake up in the morning feeling (and acting) like a bear coming out of hibernation. No one wants to cross your path, and those that do wish they had given you a wider berth.

As the day wears on, the groaning and growling even becomes a strain on you. Your mood – and your day – is getting worse; even though you didn't think that was possible. You feel a headache coming on.

When you started your journey toward a better life, you knew there would be days like this, and you prepared yourself for how to deal with it. You start rifling through your mind, past the dark clouds of gloom and doom that have surfaced, and you try to find those positive thoughts you stored away for just this occasion.

But for every positive thought you try to come up with, there's that sour disposition to shoot it down. Or maybe you can't even remember those positive thoughts and catchy affirmations you memorized.

Things are really going from bad to worse. It's on days like this that your car has a flat tire or the washing machine breaks. You have a toothache and learn you have to have a root canal. Layoffs at work mean more work for you with longer hours but the same pay. It just goes on and on. You want to go to bed and forget this day ever happened, but it's only two-thirty in the afternoon.

You get to a point where you just sit down, cross your arms on the table and lay your head down. You don't want to see what's coming next. You wonder how things could have gotten so terribly bad so terribly fast. You've been working hard to attain your dream life. You've stepped out of your comfort zone and you've battled through the unknown. You've challenged yourself and you've made the effort toward a better life. It's not fair. You don't deserve this. What is happening?

We all have days like this. You're not the only person in the world who has felt this way. Everyone has bad days. Sometimes everyone feels hopeless. Just remember, it's not the end of the world. Your bad mood and bad experiences will pass. Brighter days are just ahead.

As much as we hate feeling this way, it really moves us closer to living our dream life. How? It teaches us endurance. It tests our willpower. It's a vital step on our journey. If the caveman just sat down and gave up when he couldn't find food, we wouldn't be here. Perseverance; determination; action in the face of challenge. These are the qualities we strengthen when a bad day rolls around.

But how do we find the strength in the midst of a chaotic day? Take a lesson from a little girl in a sundress and flip flops. You smile. You say to yourself "The world may not belong to me today, but tomorrow – the world is mine." Smile even when you don't want to. Even when you have to stand in front of a mirror and take both your hands and push that smile in place.

When things go wrong, just laugh to yourself and say; "What are the odds that all of this could happen in one day?" Once you remind yourself that days like this are not the norm and that it's actually a good thing, you start to "lighten up". And when you lighten up, things lighten up as well. Things won't magically fall into place, but they won't fall apart either.

I'm betting that by the end of the day, if you consciously practice your perseverance and determination, your dark mood will have lifted and you'll awake the next morning with a better outlook. And just like that little girl, you'll feel like the world belongs to you. You'll walk around with that heart-lifting smile and infect everyone you see!

# DARE AT THE FAIR

My husband and I have been going to the State Fair for the last five years. We have a grand time, just the two of us, and even though things don't change that much, we still enjoy going.

Every year I play one game at the Midway. You take this rubber hammer and try to bounce a rubber chicken into a moving pot. Well, every year I miss. It all started when my husband dared me to play, but it's become my yearly mission to get the chicken in the pot. This year, we got to the fair and spent our usual full day walking around the exhibits, eating corn dogs, listening to the live bands and watching the parade. At the end of the day, we walked down the Midway. Just when I thought they had done away with the "chicken booth", we saw it, near the end. I walked up pulling my saved money out of my pocket while my husband stood back to watch, smiling and shaking his head.

I gave the lady my money and placed a rubber chicken on the rubber chicken hurler with sweaty hands. I'd been planning this moment for weeks, rehearsed in my mind how I was going to do it. Wait until the pot got to a certain point and then make my move. I was on a mission; I had a plan and the determination to get the job done. I knew I could do it, I could feel victory. This would be the year!

I slammed the hammer down and the rubber chicken went flying through the air. Down it came with lightning speed, just past the pot. Darn, a miss. I realigned the rubber chicken hurler, took aim and watched that rubber chicken soar through the air and land SMACK in the pot! Both my arms flew into the air – VICTORY! The lady told me that if I tried again, I could win a bigger prize if I got another one.

She tucked my money into her bag and handed me three more rubber chickens. My adrenalin was pumping and the hammer came down hard. A miss. Then another miss. Only one chicken left. I could feel the pressure building. "Take a deep breath," I told myself. I exhaled and spread my feet apart, just a hair, so my balance was perfect. I picked up the hammer, holding it with both hands, flexing my fingers to get a good grip. Taking careful aim, I sent the rubber chicken flying through the air, up, up, up then down, down, down – right into the moving pot! Needless to say, I jumped for joy as the lady handed me my prize. I walked away a winner, proudly carrying my chicken hat for all to see.

*** 

It took me five years of trying to win at that game. But here's the thing – it was a "journey". The first couple of years, it was just fun to try. Then it became more of a challenge. The fourth year is when I became determined, watched more closely and built a strategy. Weeks before we went to the fair that fifth year, I envisioned myself playing the game and seeing the chicken fall into the pot. I would rehearse it time and again in my mind. And when I got there, I knew what I was going to do. I was ready.

After the first win, I was encouraged to "keep trying for a bigger prize". Now I wasn't born yesterday and I know the lady had been trained to get people to "try again" because it meant more money for the booth. I could have walked away, but I chose to stay and go further. But I did it because *I wanted to*. I wanted to surpass the victory and prove to myself that I could get another win. I was confident that since I'd done it before, I could do it again and get a bigger prize. But the real reward was "getting there". The real reward was deciding I wanted to do it, studied the game, envisioned success and then ultimately, achieved success.

It's the same in any goal you set for yourself. You have a vision of your dream life, but you're not quite there yet. You've got to stop "playing" and make it a challenge to achieve. Be determined not to let anything stop you, strategize and envision yourself living it. But if you think reaching the goal, living your dream life, is the only prize, you're mistaken.

You see, there are rewards sprinkled throughout your path to "getting there". Living your dream life is your ultimate goal, and when you get there, it *is* a prize worth having. But you didn't just wake up one morning and say "Oh, here's my dream life!" You had to work hard and face challenges to achieve it. But you don't have to work without seeing results along the way.

Every time you take a step, you get a reward: The courage you mustered to step out and try something new. The stamina you developed as you worked your way to your ultimate goal. The knowledge you gained as you took each step of the way. And the confidence you have in yourself knowing that with each successful step, you can take another one.

When I won at that game, I didn't yell out "I got a chicken hat!"

I yelled out "I DID IT!"

And you can do it too.

# DÉJÀ VU

The other day I was at the mall, sitting on one of those concrete things in the center, having a snack. I was trying to relax, because shopping is very serious work. I kept hearing this baby crying. At first I didn't think anything of it, but the poor child kept wailing in misery. I finally turned around toward the noise (trying to be nonchalant) and realized the cause of this child's agony. It was almost Easter and "lo and behold" if the Easter Bunny wasn't sitting right there in the center of our mall having "It's" picture made with all the little children. This baby was sitting in the arms of Bunny, dressed in Easter's finest, screaming at the top of her lungs. The first adult I saw was "Grandpa" making faces and smiling at the little cherub, trying to distract her long enough for a decent shot. There was quite a crowd, each awaiting their own turn for pictures with Bunny, and everyone joined in to help. The attempt was futile; all that this baby wanted was to be in the loving arms of Mommy or Daddy.

I had to laugh to myself as I remembered back at all the times I had done the very same thing, wishing deep down that my own little blessing would miraculously stop crying, her face would return to the proper color and a big smile would appear, reflecting her delight in the moment. But just like everyone else, I have my own collection of "crying baby with Bunny; crying baby with Santa" pictures.

And every time I pull them out, I say "Oh, I remember that day…"

Recently, I had to attend meetings at our corporate headquarters, and upon seeing the "Easter baby" today, I had a twisted case of déjà vu. For anyone who has actually gone to meetings and tried to climb the "corporate ladder", you know what I'm talking about. There you are in Corporate America, dressed in your finest business attire. Some big guy in a suit is promising you something sweet if you'll just smile and be agreeable, while everyone around you is secretly making faces and smiling at you. You're confused, the pressure is building, and you feel the collar of your shirt getting tighter around your neck. You feel like screaming, wishing you were *anywhere* else but here; just like that first time you had to sit on Santa's lap…those long-felt emotions come surging back . . . WOW. . . I don't know about you, but I'm calling my mother!

***

When you actively start pursuing your dream life or your dream job, there are going to be times when you feel uncertain, when all you want to do is turn and run. When it happens, you need to realize that it's really a good thing to feel the pressure. That means you're making progress. You're never going to get where you want to go without stepping out of your comfort zone and exploring the unknown. As long as you've got a road map, you won't get lost.

If you have someone in your life you can turn to, someone you trust to listen and not try to steer you in the direction *they* want you to go, ask for a little face time with them. Talk out your fears. Just by voicing your concerns you can determine if they're real or if you're just setting up roadblocks to stay in your comfort zone. Don't let the "what if's" get you.

Maybe you don't have anyone you can turn to that is supporting you in your efforts to build a better life for yourself. Don't let that stop you. You don't have to have a fan base to achieve your life goals. You are your own support team; a leader of one. Set up small goals and cheer at your own victories.

Sometimes you're going to mess up. You're going to say the wrong thing. You're going to make a bad decision. Nobody wants to make mistakes. We want to be right all the time. But you can't. And the good news is that *nobody can.* When you remember that everyone makes mistakes (even your mentors), it's a consolation to know that you're not alone. The people you admire who have achieved what you want will openly admit to making mistakes, lots of them. And you can't get to where you want to be without making mistakes of your own. If you never mess up, you're not trying hard enough.

Even though you were scared and confused, you survived those "Santa" and "Bunny" pictures when you were a child. Sure, you screamed and cried and your face turned red, and you thought your whole world was crumbling around you - *but you survived.* In a year or two, you realized that Santa and Bunny were pretty cool after all. You couldn't wait to sit on Santa's lap and tell him what you wanted. You weren't scared any more.

And as an adult, when you have those moments of twisted déjà vu, you'll survive again. *And again.* When you're stepping out into unfamiliar territory, it's going to get a little scary sometimes. When that happens, scream and cry till your face turns red if you must, but go ahead and face it. Pull out your dream life wish list and remind yourself of how badly you want it. Then keep going.

# FRAZZLED

What should we talk about today?  Should we talk about how mad I am at my husband?  Why the dog won't eat?  The fact that my allergy medication wore off before the promised 12 hours of relief?  Why there is always so much laundry to do?  Why my car has started spitting and groaning at me?  Why it is that even though I claim to live a "simple" life, it seems so complicated?

Tonight I'm alone in the house.  I've been looking forward to a nice, quiet evening; doing only the things I want to do.  Read a good book, soak in a hot bath with lots of bubbles, veg out on the couch in front of the television; maybe write a letter or two.

Walking in the house, the first thing I do is trip over dirty clothes piled in the floor beside the washer.  Next, the phone rings.  The animals are waiting to be fed (the dog already with the look of distaste on his face) and the trash needs to be taken out.  Then there's the mail to go through and the budget to review.  Bills to be paid, but wait, the phone rings again.  Oh yeah, those birthday presents need to be wrapped and the dishwasher emptied.  Another load of clothes in the washer, a shirt that needs mending and yet another phone call.  I take a minute to push a dvd into the recorder and slip into my flannel house pants and t-shirt.  That project for work needs attention and by now I can see that my bubble bath is a distant dream.  With less than half of my list marked off, I'm already exhausted.

So what should we talk about?  Let's talk about being frazzled.  I have a dictionary with pages that are yellowed with age that states the definition of "frazzled" as "to wear to tatters; to tire out".  That's me tonight: worn to tatters and tired out, complete with drooped shoulders and dragging feet.  My shirt has a hole in it and I don't even care anymore.  I'm frazzled.

Be it exhaustion or the mere act of admitting it, once I get past the anger of my "perfect night" being ruined, I can almost laugh about it.  Saying "I'm frazzled" is much better than saying "I'm exhausted."  Exhausted sounds hopeless, while frazzled implies that I'm tired, I'm worn out, but there's still hope for me.  Being frazzled means I can slouch in a chair for a few minutes and catch my breath and still recover what's left of my sanity.  I can take a minute to remind myself that I shouldn't take things so seriously.  Yes, earlier I was pretty angry, but now I realize that the stuff on my list just isn't that important, not enough to get me in the state I was in.

On the other hand, sometimes it's fun to get frazzled, like the night before you leave on vacation.  Is everything done?  Have you packed everything you could possibly need?  Does the car have a full tank of gas?  Do you have the airline tickets?  Money?

Or how about when you're having friends and family over for the holiday? Is the house clean? Did you remember everything at the store? How long do you cook the brisket or how often do you baste the turkey? Did you put the sage in the dressing?

Yes, sometimes it's fun, even exciting to be frazzled, but tonight, for me, it's not. So I choose to be "un-frazzled" for the rest of the night. Yes, it's that easy. I'm just making a decision to not fret over all these things that have been bothering me. I'm choosing to "disconnect". The things on my list will have to wait; I'm taking a bubble bath.

* * *

Sometimes life can be daunting. Just the everyday struggles we go through is enough to make us want to collapse, both physically and emotionally, into the nearest escape hatch we can find. And when you tack on the challenges of pursuing your dream life – well, sometimes you just can't. It's not in you. You need a break.

That's all true, except that your dream life is still in you. You can't run away from it because it was born with you. It's still in there, waiting to become your reality. You still want it, but just not today – not at this moment.

You're tired. You've been working hard. You've been maintaining life's demands plus working toward your dream life. And you've made progress. But lately it's gotten harder. You're pace has slowed. Now you just feel like you're going through the motions without the emotions. You keep going, one step, two steps – but it just doesn't mean the same. Your thoughts keep telling you to keep going, don't stop. You're frazzled and it becomes one step, stumble, one step, stumble.

*The only thing you get when you beat a dead horse is a beaten up dead horse.*

You don't have to beat yourself up for wanting a break. Go ahead, have some fun – you've earned it. Get some rest, clear your mind, relax your body. The path to your dream life will be waiting for you when you get back.

The best way to avoid burn out like this is to take a break *every day*. For thirty minutes every day, do something that's just for you. Something that you can do for you alone that will help rejuvenate your body and mind. A hot bubble bath or steamy shower? A good book? A little tv time vegged out on the couch?

It's not selfish. It's necessary. Consider it part of a healthy lifestyle. It's important to appreciate yourself and the work you do. You owe it to yourself. You're probably asking yourself: *"Is it really okay to treat myself every day without feeling guilty?"* Cover your ears because I'm screaming a resounding "YES!"

Try it for one week. Every day, take thirty minutes and do something just for you. Something that makes you feel good. A way to tell yourself: "Good Job!" And during that thirty minutes, really experience the pleasure it brings you. If a long hot shower is your treat for the day, just stand there completely still and feel the hot water cascading down your body from your head to your feet – washing away all the cares of the day. The smell of the soap, clean and refreshing, that symbolizes the beginning of a fresh new start. *Learn to be in the moment and truly experience it.* If thoughts creep into your mind, push them aside. This is your time, your moment. Just think about how wonderful it feels to reward yourself to indulge in something that's just for you. Let yourself enjoy it, it's okay.

At the end of the week, reflect back and see how much easier it was to face your daily challenges with a better frame of mind, knowing that at the end of the day, you were in for a special treat from yourself. And in the pursuit of your dream life, you might have had new ideas to get you there faster. You found renewed strength and energy and focus. You're on your way again, your passion is back and you're ready to make the world a better place.

Do this every day from now on and you'll find that you don't suffer the severe burnout that you used to. The path you take in life will still have its bumps and curves, but you'll be better able to deal with them. You're un-frazzled and unstoppable.

You control your destiny.  How long you're away depends on you.

We'll be waiting.  Enjoy!

# FUZZY

Living in the country, we never have a shortage of strays (definition: animals that people dump in the country at friendly looking houses). I apparently have one of those "friendly looking houses" and recently a skinny, disheveled tabby cat wandered into my backyard.

Not being the kind of person who can see a starving animal and not feed it, I fed it. Of course, after the first bite, this creature had found a new home and has eagerly waited each day to see the bowl fill again with cat food. The only problem was that this cat was wild. I couldn't get near her without a hiss and growl.

Well, you can't feed a cat without giving it a name, so, considering the condition she was in when she found me, I named her Fuzzy. Certain I was intended to be the next Cat Whisperer, I decided to make friends. Faithfully, twice a day I filled the bowl and talked to her while she ate. Within a couple of weeks, she had put on weight, enough so that her belly protruded nicely. Her fur (hair, whatever) had smoothed out and looked silky and shiny...of course I couldn't touch her, what with her being wild and all. I thought about changing her name to Silky, but I only got that nasty hiss when I called her that so I stuck with Fuzzy.

I was content to watch her from afar, giving up my aspiration of Cat Whisperer, and enjoyed the decreased mouse population, wondering how she could possibly eat so much. A few weeks later, I found out why. Fuzzy had kittens, five little fuzzy kittens – just like her. I went from buying four-pound bags of cat food to seventeen-pound bags. Now, as I said earlier, you can't feed a cat without giving it a name, so now I have Fuzzy, Slinky, Zena, Sheba, Gabby and Fluffy.

Always up for a new challenge, I tried to tame the kittens so I could give them away to good homes. They're about half grown now and as of this date, I still have Fuzzy, Slinky, Zena, Sheba, Gabby and Fluffy. While they love to play with the feather on a pole I bought them, they refuse to be petted. I'm encouraged that they run up to see me when I go outside and when I ask who is ready for supper, I get a chorus of meows as I lead the way to the food bowl. I haven't seen a mouse in months and their antics keep me laughing non-stop.

I did end up changing Fuzzy's name to Floozy. You guessed it, she's been eating an awful lot lately and her belly is protruding nicely. I better come up with some more names real quick!

***

Sometimes, by no fault of your own, things get dumped on you. I'm not talking about the things you see coming like an increased workload when Jimmy gets fired. I'm talking about the things that blind-side you, the things you never see coming, the ones that take your organized, peaceful life and scramble it all up.

Instead of saying: "Oh crap, why did this have to happen?" take on a new perspective. Try saying: "Well, I wasn't expecting this! Here's a new challenge for me."

Before you think I'm going all Pollyanna on you, I know that your first instinct is to say: "Oh crap, why did this have to happen?" Me too. I don't like having my little world rocked around either, but it does give us an opportunity to explore a new way of looking at things – and of looking at ourselves.

The next time you get something dumped on you, I'd like you to consider your options. Look at the situation and determine every avenue available that would move that boulder out of your way, but also look to see if maybe this boulder might have some benefit to it. Maybe there are hieroglyphics on it. All you have to do is decipher it and contemplate the message. It might be that next step on the path to your dream life – an epiphany so to speak.

Maybe the cosmos is saying: "You could use some help on your way, here's a little message for you." Or, "Hey, wake up, you're going the wrong way. Don't make me drop another boulder on you!"

Either way, life is trying to tell us something. To get it, we've got to examine it. When that skinny tabby cat showed up on my doorstep, I'll be honest, my first thought was: "Great, another starving stray." But I considered my options. I didn't want another cat, but I took another look anyway. My next thought was: "It's starving; I've got to feed it."

And you know what? It turns out that I did the right thing. I saved this poor misfortunate creature from certain death by feeding her. In turn, she took care of the mice population and her kittens afforded me hours of entertainment with their happy frolicking. Not a bad trade-off!

I'm not saying that every boulder is going to have a positive benefit, but one thing I do believe is that it has a message for you. Slow down. Contemplate it. Consider your options. Determine which path you're going to take. Embrace it or maneuver around it. It will lead you where you need to go.

# GORGEOUS

I woke up the other morning and decided to watch the local news while I had my first cup of coffee. It just so happened that they were in the "fitness" segment of the broadcast. Their guest was a man from the local fitness center and he was demonstrating exercises that would get you back in shape. He had what appeared to be a jump rope, but it was really a stretchy cord with handles. He did a few exercises and I thought "Hmmm, that looks like something I could do..." Firing me up into "get fit" mode, I couldn't wait to get to the store that day after work to buy one of those stretchy cords. They had a three-pack with an instruction booklet and dvd.

Perfect! I went straight to the checkout counter, quite proud of my find, happily paid the $25 and took it home. Slipping into my sweat pants, I popped the dvd into the player and started pulling out the cords. I was pumped and ready to whip my old body back into shape.

The girl on the dvd (gorgeous, of course) is showing me how to do the first exercise, but first I have to learn the "correct posture". Okay, no problem. Hips forward, shoulders back, chin tucked, stomach in...for a minute I thought I'd bought a training video for the Army!

Okay, once I'm in the right posture, I grab one of the cords, trying to keep up with Gorgeous, except I forgot to take them out of the package first. I ripped the plastic off one and quickly returned to the correct posture, except Gorgeous had already started without me. I placed my feet on the center of the cord, just like her. Gorgeous takes this cord by the handles and effortlessly raises her arms up to her ears, flashing a brilliant smile.

Being the eager student, I put a handle in each hand and mimic her moves, except my arms only go up to my hips! "Man, I'm in worse shape than I thought!" My arms were quivering from my wrists to my shoulders, but I couldn't budge another inch. Just as a groan escaped my lips and my life flashed before my eyes, I realized I had the wrong cord! It seems that the "red handle" cord is for the advanced student.

By the time I got the beginner's cord and assumed the correct posture, Gorgeous had already floated through four more exercises. Now not being one to give up easily, I wipe the sweat from my brow, restart the video, get into position, and (I swear, it was as if Jack LaLane himself had smiled upon me), my arms went out even with my hips, up to my waist, and then my shoulders. At that point, I was so proud of myself, my muscles responding (there's the burn I've always heard people talk about!), that I decided I'd gone high enough. Hold, 2, 3, 4 – Down, 2, 3, 4.

I sailed through the rest of the video with such confidence that when I was through, I went to the mirror to admire my newly developed arm muscles and flash my own brilliant smile. If I kept this up, I could look just like

Gorgeous in no time! But wait; standing in front of the mirror, nothing looked different. Hmmm, it looks like it's going to take a little longer than I had hoped. I know, tomorrow I'll go buy a treadmill!

***

It's important that we strive to improve both our physical and mental selves. With each improvement we make, we're one step closer to living our dream lives. Who doesn't want to be attractive and smart, right? It's just an obvious fact that we include those traits with our dream lives.

By all means, spend some time every day working both your physical and mental muscles. But don't make the big mistake of trying to be someone else. Work on being a better you, not to be like Gorgeous in my fitness dvd.

When we try to be like someone else, we lose our own identity, and the chance for our dream life flies right out the window. We've traded it for the hopes of being someone else. Their lives look more glamorous than ours. They have it all, good looks, nice house, fancy car. We want that too!

But you don't get it by copying others. When you admire someone, turn them into a mentor, not an idol. Learn what it took for them to get where they are today. Then turn back to yourself and figure out what it would take for you to do it too. You don't have to turn yourself into them to get what they have. Take some time to consider your options. Plan your route. You may be surprised to learn that you have a better way of getting there than they did! You've got the secret formula for being the best person you can be, to live that dream life – just like you've imagined, or better!

Stop chasing shadows and step into the spotlight. Show us how awesome you are!

# GRANDMAS AND MINIVANS

It's summer and school is out, which means it's time for the grandchildren (all four of them) to visit for a week. We have one granddaughter, age fifteen, and three grandsons, one is eleven and the other two are eight. Now, I'm not the average grandmother that sits around knitting and filling the house with the smell of fresh baked bread. I'm more of a "let's go to town" and "don't walk on the couch" grandmother. My husband wants to buy a minivan, but I won't do it because I don't want the "grandma" reputation. Minivans are for "soccer moms" and "grandmothers" and I'm too old to be considered a soccer mom but not old enough for the grandmother status either!

The first day was spent in chaos, light sabers swinging through the house, a video blaring on the tv, toys scattered all over the house, and me with a cold compress over my face. By the second day, I had adjusted and realized that "quiet time" was going to be next week at the soonest. The washer ran almost the entire day and I moved from the stove to the icebox nonstop. We barbequed and put up the pool in the backyard. It was so late by then that we didn't get to swim, but tomorrow was coming. I had to work half a day and on my way home, I stopped at my "always" store for milk and other basic "stay alive" sundries. When I got home, I walked in the door and said "I'm home" and all four kids jumped up and cheered. Even Grandpa mumbled a word of thanks. Something inside me grew warm and happy. As I was unloading my bags, I said "Look what they put in my bag!" and pulled out two floatation rings and a beach ball. "Let's go swimming!" I yelled and everyone scattered to find their swimsuits.

By the third day, I had it down pat: grilled cheese for breakfast, Cheetos for lunch and we go to town for supper. The freezer was packed with ice cream for after swimming and popcorn and videos at night. I learned that transformers like to play with the sesame street characters and that plastic cars are great tub toys. I learned that my grandson can draw an awesome cat and that everyone gets a big laugh out of watching me play video games. It seems that my video character can only walk into walls while theirs can climb them, and for some reason that is extremely funny.

By the fourth day, I learned how to maneuver through the house without stepping on toy soldiers while carrying an armful of dirty clothes. I learned that my granddaughter likes bookstores as much as I do and that Grandpa can fall asleep holding a cup of coffee.

Before I knew it, the week had come to an end. It had been wild and crazy at times, but it had been great. I was afraid that I would be exhausted by the end of the week, but honestly, I had never felt more alive. Being a grandmother doesn't mean that you're old, it means that you can have fun again. After this week, I may have to rethink that minivan reputation, but right now, I need to look for the cat, I haven't seen her in days!

\*\*\*

You know what kind of life you want to have. You're out there every day working to make it a reality. But while you're traveling that road to your dream life, don't make the mistake of being too hard on yourself. Don't make a mold for yourself so rigid that you can't break out of it. When you're faced with life's challenges you're going to have to bend a little sometimes. You're going to have to step out of that cast you've made for yourself and do a little adjusting.

Your road to a better life is not straight. It's got twists and turns in it, and you've got to be flexible enough to stay on course. Traveling toward your dream life means you have to make changes before you can move away from where you are now.

Things aren't always going to turn out the way you want them to. You've got to realize that right from the start. The challenge lies in how you respond to those changes. You may see that bump in the road before you get to it, or you might have been looking at the scenery and not seen it coming. Either way, you're going to have to deal with it. You can either say "Someone should fix that bump, it jarred my teeth out when I hit it", or you can say "Woo Hoo! That was something else! I better keep my eyes on the road so I'll see the next one coming."

Change isn't always bad. As a matter of fact, when you're hot on the trail of your dream life, changes are the road signs that point you in the right direction - that let you know you're making progress. As your situations change, you have to change with them. That's how you get there.

Look at the new challenges that face you. Examine them closely. Decide which road is the best to take to overcome them. You may have to slow down when those bumps appear and work a little harder than usual to get past them. Or you may decide to just roll down the windows and let the wind blow through your hair as you fly over them. Whichever you choose, be flexible enough to grow from the experience.

It doesn't matter whether you're driving a minivan or a sports car, there are always going to be bumps in the road to your dream life. And while you're maneuvering around them, don't forget to enjoy the scenery (and if you see my cat, would you tell her it's safe to come home?).

# HEAD BANGING

Okay, picture this: It's Monday morning, it's raining and the traffic is worse than frustrating. Road construction again. The person in front of me is going fifty on the highway and the person behind me is polishing the chrome of my bumper with their license plate. I take my usual exit ramp only to come to a screeching stop at the "always red when I get there" light. One of my wiper blades flops on each swipe across the windshield. I haven't seen the sun in over a week and my mood is as gray as the sky above me. The only thing worse than having to get out in this weather is realizing that the weekend is over and it's time to go back to work. I would much rather have stayed at home, nice and warm in my blankets, listening to the coffee brew.

I take a swig from my travel mug and look in the rearview mirror. There's a guy behind me, I would guess around forty-ish in a suit and tie sitting behind the wheel of his car, get this – head banging. Does this guy not realize it's Monday morning, it's raining, this light will never turn green and my windshield wiper is flopping? How could he possibly be head banging on a Monday morning? What kind of music has he got anyway? Zeppelin? The Stones? I look away just checking to see of the "I'll turn green when I'm good and ready" light has changed yet. It hasn't. I look to the side, rain. I watch my wiper flop. I look into the rearview mirror again. He's still head banging and this time, upon closer inspection, I see he's singing. I think to myself "Who head bangs any more anyway?" I haven't head banged since I was a teenager. "What's with this guy?"

I can't help but chuckle as I watch him. It brings back memories. I start looking through my cd collection for my own "head banging" music. Hmmm. Willie Nelson – no, Norah Jones, no – Burl Ives Christmas – what's THAT doing in here? Ah-Ha! Fleetwood Mac! Yeah, that'll do! I pop it into the player, crank up the volume and put both hands on the steering wheel, ready to head bang! My wiper keeps perfect time with the music. The light finally turns green and I'm on my way again. I take one last look into the rearview mirror. Thanks Buddy, for reminding me that there's a better way to bang my head on a Monday morning.

***

Sometimes it seems like everything is going wrong. One little thing piles on to another little thing, then another little thing, and before you know it you're having a bad day. All you can see is the bad. If you do happen to see any good, it's happening to someone else – and that's bad. That dream life of yours is just that – a dream. When everything starts getting in the way it makes you feel hopeless and you start to consider giving up on your dreams. It's like everything in the world is trying to stop you.

Here are a few suggestions to help you turn things around:

**Get mad.** Take the attitude that no matter what happens, you're not going to quit. You're going to fight. Every little thing (or big thing) that gets in your path to that dream life is going to fuel your energy to succeed. With every roadblock you face, it will give you more determination to keep going. "You think you can keep me from achieving my dreams? Bring it on! I'm ready. Everything you can throw at me will just make me stronger and more determined to succeed. You think road construction on a rainy Monday morning is going to stop me? Think again."

Do this with each obstacle that threatens to weaken your resolve. Now be clear, I'm not talking about getting mad and confronting someone you feel has wronged you. I'm talking about the things that crop up and alter your plans. Say you were going to spend the evening painting that masterpiece but you ended up having to work late. When you got home one of your water pipes broke and your bathroom was flooded. You had to spend that time cleaning up and replacing the pipes. You're thinking: "That figures, on the night I finally decide to paint my masterpiece my pipes break. I've been planning this for weeks. Karma's trying to tell me I'm not supposed to do it." You're mad. Instead of using that anger to discourage you, *change the way you think of getting mad.* "I can't paint my masterpiece because of this, but you mark my words, I'm going to paint! It may not be tonight, it may not be tomorrow night, but I WILL PAINT! If I have to, I'll paint one blade of grass a day, but that masterpiece WILL get done!" Take that Karma!

**Be glad.** When you start to notice that things are blocking your path to a better life - that means you're on the right track. Before you decided to fulfill your dreams, you never really took those obstacles seriously. They were just part of life, one of those things that happen. Before, you might have told your friends: "I came home the other night and my pipes in the bathroom were broken. It took me all night to clean up and replace those pipes. What a mess!" But now you're taking them personally. "I had to put off painting my masterpiece to fix those pipes." You've got plans for your future and you're working toward your dream life. You're beginning to notice when something knocks you off course and you're learning how to deal with it. You're on your way!

**Lighten up and look at the big picture.** When you get further down the road to your dream life, you're going to look back at all the obstacles you faced along the way. Sometimes you're going to think: "Boy, I really nailed that one!" And other times it will be: "I made a mess of that. I can see *now* how I could have handled it much better." They are the lessons you learned along the way that will help you make better choices in the future. The obstacles you're facing right now are the things that are going to make you a better person. So that when you finally reach that dream life, you'll be ready for it. And for those times that you feel like banging your head, remember to turn on some music first!

# HEADS OR TAILS

When our daughter asked if she could move back home, her father and I welcomed her with open arms; arms that were quickly filled with the personal belongings in the back of her truck and her three most prized possessions: her dog, cat and fish. Well, we weren't prepared for a small menagerie, but with the pleading look on her face we reluctantly conceded. The fish were no problem at all, but the other two have proven to turn this house into a circus. I'll limit this story to her dog, fondly referred to as Peabody.

Upon first glance, it was obvious that he was a cute thing, a white Chihuahua pup just eight weeks old. His eyes sparkled with youth and curiosity and as hard as I tried, I couldn't help getting attached to him. He made us all laugh at his antics and his frisky nature. I learned right away that both ends of him worked really well. Whatever he didn't bark at, he peed on. Not being housebroken, he was quickly quarantined to my daughter's bedroom, training pads covering her floor. As we waited for warm weather to come, we endured the ceaseless yapping and watched the sky for the first signs of spring.

Finally it came, and after three weeks of hard work and three hundred dollars, Peabody was introduced to his beautiful new dog kennel. It was the perfect place for him to spend the day until after a quiet supper when he would join us back in the house. It had to be sturdy, so we made it with wood and chicken wire. The door even had a small opening at the bottom with a latch so we could access the kennel easily. It even had a roof so he would have shade and protection from the outside cat, which I have no doubt would practice her own cunning on him.

I was so happy to come home to peace and quiet. I could eat supper without the incessant yapping and my house didn't have that "new dog smell". I was thrilled, to say the least. I even commented to my husband how wonderful it was, and that I thought everything would turn out fine from now on.

My joy was short-lived when a few days later my daughter discovered a rash on the pup. His whole belly was covered. Off he went to the vet and my daughter called me as soon as she got the news. "He's allergic to grass!" I nearly fell out of my chair. Of all the dogs in the world, this one in particular was allergic to grass! How could a dog be allergic to grass anyway? He was on medicine for two weeks and had to stay indoors. I felt a migraine coming on and it lasted just about two weeks! With a clean bill of health, we decided to try the kennel again. This time we put down a floor. I waited with bated breath each day, praying that the rash wouldn't reappear. Thankfully, it didn't.

One day my husband and I were working in the yard and decided to let him out to get some exercise. I looked up to see him chasing the chickens. They ran around the side of the house and as I started yelling and running to get him, they re-emerged, this time the chickens chasing the dog! This was another important lesson I learned about Chihuahuas that day – they love to be chased! We have ten acres and I chased him over the whole thing. He wasn't satisfied with that though, he ran over to the neighbor's place and found horse pooh. It was fresh and he couldn't resist the urge to roll in it. As I called him from the fence line, he grabbed a piece of dried pooh which he carried with him as our chase resumed. He would chew on it whenever I stopped to catch my breath. I could tell he was enjoying country life by the way he would wag his tail just before he darted out of my reach. Upon seeing him with green horse pooh stains on both sides of his head and neck and a half-eaten horse pooh in his mouth, I really didn't want to catch him, but I could see my daughter's face if anything happened to him and that urged me on.

Finally, after about ten more heart pounding minutes, I nabbed the little devil and carried him at arm's length straight to the bathtub. He stood regally while I washed him, green water sliding down the drain. Thanks to his antics, I now had to clean the bathtub as well. He was certain he won the race and I was certain never to let him out of that kennel again without a leash.

On the up side, he is a wonderful watchdog. The slightest noise brings him to full attention and if ever a hapless burglar were to wander into our house, I'm sure

Peabody would do everything in his power to protect us. If he didn't pierce the intruder's eardrums from the shrill barking, he'd definitely pee on him.

*  *  *

Have you been dreaming of a better life but haven't taken action to make it a reality? Is it because you're afraid you may fail? Are you afraid of making mistakes? Think you're not smart enough? Maybe you're afraid you'll embarrass yourself.

If that's the case, I've got good news for you. You don't need to worry about any of that stuff! Just close your eyes to all of the reasons that are holding you back and take one step toward your dream. When you take that first step, something happens inside you. Yes, you may be afraid and you may get sweaty palms, but you're also going to get a rush of excitement. You're going to get a surge of confidence. You're going to want to take another step.

You're going to realize that yes, you *will* make some mistakes along the way – but not every step is a mistake. You're going to keep taking steps, faster and faster, until you find yourself running toward that dream. Somewhere in the midst of all those steps is the point where you say "I'm not turning back." That's when you feel the thrill of the chase.

That's you – chasing after the dream that's been out of your reach. The one you've longed for your whole life.  You feel the excitement flowing through every fiber of your being; the anticipation of living the life of your own choosing.  You're doing it – you're running the race that is your destiny.

Never lose sight of your dream.  There will be times when it seems almost within reach and others when it seems distant and untouchable.  Just keep running toward it.

I chose the story of Peabody because it's a perfect example of what I'm trying to share with you.  He didn't hold himself back.  He just took off running.  Yes, he got chased by some angry chickens and even ended up with pooh all over him, but that didn't stop him.  You see, his dream was to be free, and as long as he was running, he *was* free.

As long as you are actively pursuing your dream you are living it.  You're running toward it, you see it every day.  It becomes a part of you.  You can feel it.

Eventually, with training, Peabody learned that he could be free to run around on his own.  He could explore every inch of our place and still enjoy the company of his humans.  His dream came true.  He was free.

You can be free too.  Learn what it takes to achieve your dream, and then enjoy the thrill of the chase to get it.  Just remember that if you happen to get in a little pooh, it washes right off!

# WHAT'LL IT BE?

Paper or plastic? Coffee or tea? Regular or Decaf? Sweet or Unsweet? Debit or Credit? White or Wheat? Large or Small? These are just a few of the decisions I make each day. They are small choices I make that show what my preferences are. My mother always said, "You always have a choice." Of course she was referring more to the tougher decisions in life, and that's what I've been thinking about lately.

Lead or follow? Win or Lose? Weak or Strong? Help or Hinder? Right or Wrong? Each day, we all wake up and begin making decisions. Cereal or eggs for breakfast? Brown or black pants? Scenic or direct route to work? Still, all minor choices. At what point during the day do we begin making those tougher choices? Sadly, some of us never do. We let the minor ones fill our days so we don't have to think about the tougher ones.

I'm sure you've heard the old saying: "Lead, follow or get out of the way!" Too many of us just get out of the way, we just step back and watch all the leaders and followers go by. We envy the leaders and make fun of the followers. When they've all passed us by, what have we got? "Coffee, decaf with a wheat bagel please". That's right; we've still got our minor choices.

When geese migrate, there's always a leader and they fly in a V formation. When the leader gets tired, it drops back and another goose takes its place and the flock has a new leader. It's not that the leader is the only one who knows how to get there; it's just the one that flew off first. And when all the geese finally get to their destination, they enjoy the warm sun on their feathers and eat gooseberry pie on the beach. What about the goose who just got out of the way? It's cold and lonely. "Should I get in the water or stay out? Should I take a nap or get something to eat?" That's right; it's busy making its minor choices. And while it's sitting around thinking, it gets grabbed up and becomes Thanksgiving dinner! The moral of the story is this: Stop busying yourself with minor choices, spread your wings; be a leader or a follower, but don't just "be". Do something before your goose gets cooked!

*\*\**

We are all leaders when we step up to a challenge, when we finally stop thinking and spread our wings. We are winners when we make the effort and only losers when we stop trying. We give up our weakness when we say, "I'll try" and give it an honest effort and become stronger with each step we take. We learn from the wrong and celebrate the right. And when you come to an obstacle in your path, when you're stuck and don't know which way to go, just remember, "You *always* have a choice."

# Confidence and Courage

When it all boils down to it, fear is the number one reason we fail to start the journey to our dream lives. There are several different types of fear we face when we step out of our comfort zones. It doesn't matter what kind of fear you have at this point. The only thing you need to understand is that you're afraid. You don't have to name it. You don't have to analyze it. And you don't have to work your way around it.

Instead, just accept the fact that you're afraid. Admit it to yourself and acknowledge that, up to this point, it's been blocking your path to a better life. Refuse to listen to the part of you that's feeding that fear and holding you back. Stop thinking about it, it doesn't serve you anymore.

You don't have to be worried or afraid that you can't complete the whole journey. All you need to concentrate on right now is finding the courage to take that first step. With courage comes confidence. With confidence comes more courage. They go together to help you on your journey. Use courage first to get you started. Don't let fear keep you on the sidelines pining away for your dream life. Take that first step. As soon as you take action, confidence comes to your aid.

Once you have the courage to take that first step, you know with certainty that you can take another one. With each success your confidence grows, and with each misstep, your courage carries you through it. Let them work together to get you to your dream life. Just keep taking those steps until you get there.

From the moment you take that first step, you're going to feel excitement like you never have before. Instead of being idle, you're reaching out to make that dream life a reality. It's like you've only just now awakened, you're stretching yourself. You open your eyes and you can see it. It's right there! That dream life is yours – take it.

RIGHT NOW, break free of the chains that are holding you back. Don't let those tired excuses block the way for your dream life to emerge. Gather your courage and make that first step a leap – with your eyes wide open. I guarantee that you don't want to miss a second of it.

Refuse to "live a life of quiet aspiration". Cast off those limiting beliefs and feel the passion of creating your dream life. Look at the circumstances that surround you. Life has the guidebook. You choose which path to take on your journey.

*It's time to get ready, set, and stop putting off your dream life.*

72007109R00035

Made in the USA
San Bernardino, CA
21 March 2018